■SCHOLASTIC

P9-DCI-120

WITHDRAWN

Sandwich Bag Science

25 Easy, Hands-on Activities That Teach Key Concepts in Physical, Earth, and Life Sciences—and Meet the Science Standards

by Steve "The Dirtmeister®" Tomecek

New York • Toronto • London • Auckland • Sydney
New Delhi • Mexico City • Hong Kong • Buenos Aires

Teaching *Resources*

Dedication
To Joanna Shubin,
a master science teacher
who showed me the way.
Thanks!

Scholastic Inc. grants teachers permission to photocopy the reproducible pages from this book for classroom use. No other part of this publication may be reproduced in whole or in part, or stored in a retrieval system, or transmitted in any form or by any means, electronic, mechanical, photocopying, recording, or otherwise, without written permission of the publisher. For information regarding permission, write to Scholastic Inc., 557 Broadway, New York, NY 10012.

Cover and interior design by NEO Grafika Studio
Illustrations by Mike Moran

ISBN-13: 978-0-439-75466-8
ISBN-10: 0-439-75466-6
Copyright © 2006 by Steve Tomecek
All rights reserved.
Printed in the U.S.A.

3 4 5 6 7 8 9 10   40   15 14 13 12 11 10 09 08 07

Table of Contents

PHYSICAL SCIENCE

EARTH SCIENCE

Introduction

Science is not a spectator sport! For students to truly understand the concepts that make our world operate, they must be able to experiment with different phenomena. Unfortunately, science supplies can get quite expensive and, in many cases, they're not all that "kid friendly." Finding reasonably priced materials that stand up to student use can be both difficult and time consuming. That's why we've developed this series of science activity books. Like its two companions, *Coffee Can Science* and *Soda Bottle Science*, *Sandwich Bag Science* presents students with hard-core science experiences using "dirt cheap" materials.

Sandwich Bag Science features 25 standards-based science activities structured around the use of one or more empty zipper-style sandwich bags. By following the simple instructions in this book and using a few other household materials, you and your students will be able to conduct dozens of fun and easy hands-on experiments and projects related to the physical, earth, and life sciences. While some of the activities in this book have been adapted from previously published ideas, many more are original designs. They have all been developed and tested in actual classroom settings with elementary and middle-school students so you can be sure they all work. In the end, we hope that they'll not only inspire your students to learn more science, but also give you the inspiration to experiment and develop your own inexpensive science activities.

How to Use This Book

Each of the 25 activities in this book comes with its own teaching guide and reproducible lab sheet for student use. The teaching guide features background information about the key science concepts in the activity, plus a mini-lesson and demonstration to introduce students to the activity. The reproducible page offers easy step-by-step instructions on how to conduct the activity, plus critical-thinking questions that invite students to make and write their own predictions, record results, and explain the outcomes of their experiment—a great way to combine science and writing!

There are several ways you can use or present the activities in this book:

✦ Use the activities as teacher demonstrations to spark students' interest and get them revved up for an upcoming lesson on a related science topic.

✦ Have students conduct the hands-on activities as directed. To make the activity more manageable, you may want to divide the class into small groups and have students work together to do the activity.

♦ Set up "stations" around the classroom and present related activities at the same time. For example, you can present Sandwich Bag Seed Germinator (page 49), Moldy Matters (page 53), and Bags of Yeast (page 57) together and have students investigate some of the environmental factors that affect the life and growth of organisms. When you set up multiple stations around the room, students can rotate to each one and see how they all relate to the same concept.

Whichever option you choose, be sure to provide each student with his or her own copy of the lab sheet. This way, each student understands what the activity is about and can record his or her own predictions and observations.

Getting Your Bags

It goes without saying that you will need many sandwich bags to complete the activities in this book. You can either purchase boxes of bags in bulk or ask students to bring in clean, individual bags from home. Several experiments use both small sandwich bags and larger gallon-size storage bags. Most of the activities require zipper-style self-closing bags rather than the fold-top bags, so be sure to get the correct type.

For some of the activities, you will need a few basic science supplies such as magnets, iron filings, and magnifiers. Most of these materials can easily be purchased from any educational or science supply store. One excellent source of materials is Educational Innovations. To obtain a catalog, call toll-free at 888-912-7474 or visit their Web site at www.teachersource.com.

National Science Education Standards

The activities in this book meet the following science standards:

Physical Science

For Grades K–4:
Properties of Objects and Materials
- ✦ Objects have many observable properties, including temperature. Those properties can be measured using tools, such as thermometers.
- ✦ Objects can be described by the properties of the materials from which they are made.
- ✦ Materials can exist in different states—solid, liquid, and gas. Some materials can be changed from one state to another by heating or cooling.

Position and Motion of Objects
- ✦ The position of an object can be described by locating it relative to another object or background.
- ✦ The position and motion of objects can be changed by pushing and pulling. The size of the change is related to the strength of the push or pull.
- ✦ Sound is produced by vibrating objects. The pitch of a sound can be varied by changing the rate of vibration.

Light, Heat, Electricity, and Magnetism
- ✦ Light travels in a straight line until it strikes an object. It can be reflected, refracted, or absorbed.
- ✦ Heat can be produced in many ways and can move from one object to another.
- ✦ Magnets attract and repel each other and certain kinds of other materials.

For Grades 5–8:
Properties and Changes of Properties in Matter
- ✦ Substances react chemically in characteristic ways with other substances to form new substances with different properties.

Motions and Forces
- ✦ Unbalanced forces will cause changes in the speed or direction of an object's motion.

Transfer of Energy
+ Energy is a property of many substances and is associated with heat, mechanical motion, sound, and light. Energy is transferred in many ways.
+ Heat moves in predictable ways, flowing from warmer objects to cooler ones.
+ Light interacts with matter by transmission and absorption.
+ A tiny fraction of the light from the sun reaches the earth, transferring energy from the sun to the earth.

Earth and Space Science

For Grades K–4:
Properties of Earth Materials
+ Earth materials are solid rocks and soils, water and gases of the atmosphere. The varied materials have different physical and chemical properties.

Changes in the Earth and Sky
+ The surface of the earth changes. Some changes are due to slow processes such as erosion and weathering.
+ Weather changes from day to day. Weather can be described by measurable quantities, such as temperature and precipitation.

For Grades 5–8:
Structure of the Earth System
+ Some changes in the earth can be described as the "rock cycle." Old rocks at Earth's surface weather, forming sediments that are deposited and buried.
+ Water, which covers the majority of the earth's surface, circulates through the "water cycle." Water evaporates from the earth's surface, rises and cools as it moves to higher elevations, condenses, and falls back to the surface.

Life Science

For Grades K–4:
Characteristics of Organisms
+ Organisms have basic needs. Animals require air, water, and food; plants require air, water, nutrients, and light. Organisms can survive only in environments where their needs are met.
+ Each plant or animal has different structures that serve different functions in growth, survival, and reproduction.
+ The behavior of an organism is influenced by internal cues and external cues such as a change in the environment.
+ Humans and other organisms have senses that help them detect internal and external cues.

Life Cycles of Organisms
✦ Plants and animals have life cycles that include being born, developing into adults, reproducing, and dying.

Organisms and Their Environments
✦ An organism's patterns of behavior are related to the nature of that organism's environment. When the environment changes, some organisms survive and reproduce, and others die or move to new locations.
✦ All organisms cause changes in the environment where they live.

For Grades 5–8:
Structure and Function in Living Things
✦ The human organism has systems for digestion.
✦ Specialized cells perform specialized functions in multicellular organisms.

Regulation and Behavior
✦ All organisms must be able to obtain and use resources, grow, reproduce, and maintain stable internal conditions while living in a constantly changing external environment.
✦ Regulation of an organism's internal environment involves sensing the internal environment and changing physiological activities to keep conditions within a range required to survive.

Science and Technology
✦ People have invented tools and techniques to solve problems.
✦ Tools help scientists make better observations and measurements.

Leakproof Bag

Get It Together
- large rubber band
- 2-foot length of plain cotton or kite string
- "Elastic Plastic" lab sheet (page 11)

Science in the Bag

Polymers are substances made up of repeated chains of smaller molecules called *monomers*. Depending on the way these chains are assembled, polymers can be either brittle or soft. Some polymers belong to a special class of substances called *elastomers*. Elastomers, like rubber and certain plastics, can stretch and bend and then return to their original shape. These types of substances can be used to secure materials together (bungee cords and rubber bands) or to seal containers tight (cellophane wrap and sandwich bags). One of the more novel uses of elastomers is in "run flat" car tires. When a tire gets punctured, elastomers seal the hole so the driver can get to safety.

Before You Start

This activity can be done either as a hands-on activity in which students work in small groups, or as a demonstration in which each student completes his or her own lab sheet.

What to Do

❶ Inform the class that they are going to play with some miracles of modern industrial engineering called *polymers*. Explain that a polymer is a long molecule made up of many smaller molecules called *monomers* that are linked together. Point out that the prefix *poly-* means "many." While there are natural polymers, like rubber and cellulose (which is what wood is made from), most polymers we use today are synthetic and fall under the broad category of *plastics*.

❷ Ask students to think of as many things as they can that are made out of plastic. You'll end up with a very long list! Plastics are so useful because different polymers have very different properties, depending on how their molecules are assembled.

❸ Call on a student volunteer. Take a piece of string and have the student hold one end tightly. Ask the class: What will happen when we pull hard on the string? *(It will quickly break.)*

❹ After breaking the string, give the student one end of a large rubber band that has been cut. Ask: What will happen when we pull the rubber band? *(It will stretch.)*

❺ Explain that both the string and rubber band contain polymers, but the rubber band has *elastomers*, which can stretch and then return back to its original shape. Give each student a copy of the "Elastic Plastic" lab sheet, and invite them to test elastomers.

Elastic Plastic

How do elastic substances behave?

❶ Examine the sandwich bag and the cup. Both are made of plastic, which is also called a *polymer*. Briefly describe the properties of each object below:

Plastic Cup:

_____

You'll Need

- zipper-style sandwich bag
- 6-oz disposable plastic cup
- pencil with a sharp point
- water
- large dishpan or bowl

Sandwich Bag:

_____

❷ Based on your initial observations, which do you think will be the more elastic of the two? Why?

_____

❸ Fill the sandwich bag ¾ full of water and zip it tightly closed. What will happen if you jabbed a pencil into the side of the bag where the water is? Write your prediction below:

_____

❹ Grasp the bag by the zipper with one hand and hold it over a dishpan. Take the pencil in your other hand and, with a quick jab, stick the pencil right through the bag where the water is and out the other side. What happens to the water in the bag? Record your observations below:

_____

_____

❺ Now prepare to do the same thing with the plastic cup. Predict: What will happen this time?

_____

❻ Fill the cup ¾ full of water and hold it by the top rim over the dishpan or bowl. Stick the pencil into the side of the cup. What happens this time? Record your observations here:

_____

_____

❼ Based on your observations, which plastic is more elastic—the cup or the bag? How do you know?

_____

_____

Think About It: How does this experiment explain how puncture-proof tires on cars work?

Mystery Matter

Get It Together

- 1½ cup water
- 16-oz box of cornstarch
- large bowl
- zipper-style sandwich bag (for each group of students)
- spoon
- 6-oz plastic cup half-filled with frozen water
- "Slime Time" lab sheet (page 13)

Science in the Bag

Matter is always changing. When matter changes state, it's called a *physical change*. A physical change is reversible. You can take a piece of ice, melt it, collect the water, and refreeze it back to ice by changing the temperature. In theory, you can keep doing physical changes to a piece of matter indefinitely because you're not changing its composition, only its form. While most physical changes involve heat, other forms of energy can cause a physical change as well. If certain types of matter are suddenly put under pressure, they, too, can change state. In this activity, the "mystery matter," known as a *colloidal suspension*, is a thick, viscous liquid when it's not under pressure, but turns solid when squeezed.

Before You Start

Prepare the cornstarch mixture before class starts. In a large bowl, mix a 16-ounce box of cornstarch with about 1½ cups of water and mix with your hands until it is well blended. You might have to add a little extra water to keep the mixture fluid. Divide the mixture into sandwich bags, making sure to leave some "mystery matter" for your demonstration.

What to Do

❶ Hold up the clear plastic cup with frozen water. Ask students: What state of matter is the material in the cup? *(Solid)* If you want to change the solid into a liquid, what would you need to do? *(Heat the ice or let the cup sit in a warm room until the ice melts.)* Once the ice turns completely liquid, is there any way to make it solid again? *(Place the cup back into the freezer.)*

❷ Explain that when you freeze and melt a substance, you are making a physical change. In a physical change, the material doesn't change its composition, only its form. Most physical changes are reversible, and the most common ones involve adding or taking away heat.

❸ Take the bowl of "mystery matter" and scoop up a big handful. Hold your hand over the bowl and allow the matter to drip back into the bowl. Explain to students that they are going to investigate another way a physical change can happen using this "mystery matter." Give each student a copy of the "Slime Time" lab sheet and a bag of "mystery matter."

Slime Time

How can matter undergo a physical change?

You'll Need

- zipper-style sandwich bag with "mystery matter" (from your teacher)

❶ Hold the bag with the "mystery matter" flat on your hand. Allow the bag to settle. Observe the material in the bag. What does it look like? How does it feel? Record your observations below:

_____

_____

❷ Based on your observations, in what state of matter is your mystery matter? Why do you think so?

_____

_____

❸ Now take the bag with the "mystery matter" and squeeze it firmly. With your finger, poke the matter with several sharp jabs. How does it feel?

_____

_____

❹ Normally, to change the state of matter, you either heat it or cool it. In the case of the mystery matter, how are you changing its state?

_____

Think About It: Can you think of any other substances that sometimes behave like your mystery matter? Hint: It's red and tastes great on French fries.

Gas Bag

OBJECTIVE: To observe a chemical change in matter

Get It Together
- match
- candle
- "It's a Gas!" lab sheet (page 15)

Science in the Bag
Matter is always changing. A physical change, such as a change in state of matter, is reversible. When matter undergoes a *chemical change*, however, the change is permanent. A chemical change may or may not involve a change of state, but in the end, a new substance is created. One type of chemical change involves a reaction between an *acid* and a *base*. Acids are corrosive chemicals, like the sulfuric acid in a car battery. There are many weak acids, too, like vinegar, lemon juice, and tea. Soap and ammonia are examples of bases. Bases can also be weak or strong. In this particular activity, when baking soda (a base) is mixed with vinegar, carbon dioxide is formed. In addition to this new substance, there is a change in temperature. The mixture gets cold because it takes away heat from the surrounding environment. This type of reaction is called an *endothermic reaction*. More often, chemical reactions are *exothermic*—they give off heat. Burning a candle or a piece of wood is an exothermic reaction.

Before You Start
This activity can be done either as a hands-on activity in which students work in small groups, or as a demonstration in which each student completes his or her own lab sheet.

What to Do
❶ Light a candle and hold it in front of the class. Encourage students to observe the candle carefully and note all the changes taking place. (As the candle burns, it gives off light, heat, and smoke. Some wax may melt and the candle gets smaller.)

❷ Explain that, unlike a piece of ice that undergoes a physical change when it melts, the candle is undergoing a chemical change. A physical change can be reversed, while a chemical change is a one-way change.

❸ Ask: What does the candle wax turn into when it burns? *(Smoke, gas, and heat)* Explain that when things burn, they give off heat energy. This is called an *exothermic reaction*. Some chemical changes are *endothermic reactions*—they take away heat from their surroundings, so they feel cold.

❹ Ask: Can you think of other chemical changes that don't involve something burning? *(Metal rusting, acids dissolving materials, soapy water mixing with oil)*

❺ Invite students to conduct their own test of a simple chemical change. Give each student a copy of the "It's a Gas!" lab sheet.

It's a Gas!

How do substances behave when they undergo a chemical change?

❶ In this activity, you will create a simple chemical change in matter using an acid and a base. The acid is vinegar and the base is baking soda. Put on your safety goggles. Place a teaspoon of baking soda into the sandwich bag. Carefully observe the substance and describe its properties below:

_____

_____

You'll Need

- safety goggles
- zipper-style sandwich bag
- I teaspoon baking soda
- 3-oz cup of vinegar

❷ Carefully observe the vinegar and describe its properties below:

_____

_____

❸ Without spilling any of the liquid, carefully place the cup of vinegar into the bag of baking soda so that the cup is standing up inside. Zip the bag closed, making sure to seal it tightly. What do you think will happen when the two substances mix? Write your prediction here:

_____

_____

❹ Pour the vinegar into the baking soda. Make sure to hold the zipper part of the bag up. Keep your other hand on the bottom of the bag. How does the bag feel? What other changes are taking place? Record your observations below:

_____

_____

❺ Carefully observe the substances that are left in the bag now. How have they changed? Are these the same materials you started with?

_____

_____

Think About It: In this activity, you made a chemical change. How is a chemical change different from a physical change, like melting a piece of ice?

Sandwich Bag Science   Scholastic Teaching Resources

Polymers at Play

Get It Together

- 20 Mule Team® borax detergent
- bottle of white glue
- clear plastic cup
- a 3-oz paper cup filled with hardened white glue
- "Bouncing Glue Balls" lab sheet (page 17)

Science in the Bag

Some chemical changes involve a change of state or a change in energy. In the "It's a Gas!" activity (page 15), we looked at one that had both. Some chemical changes involve the reorganization of molecules into a new form, where the chemical and physical properties of the final product are nothing like the original components. In this activity, students create their own simple polymer-like substance using some common household chemicals. During the reaction, the molecules undergo a major reorganization, producing a substance with some very unusual characteristics.

Before You Start

For this activity to work properly, you need 20 Mule Team® brand borax laundry detergent, available at large supermarkets. Unfortunately there are no substitutes for this brand. Several days before you do this activity, fill a 3-ounce cup halfway with white glue and leave it standing out in the air to harden.

What to Do

❶ In front of the class, take the bottle of white glue and begin pouring it into a clear plastic cup. Ask students: What properties does the glue have? *(It's a thick liquid that is very sticky.)*

❷ Next, pass around the cup of glue that you allowed to harden. Ask: What properties does this glue have? *(It's hard, brittle, and solid.)*

❸ Explain that when the glue was left out in the air, it underwent a chemical change. A *chemical change* is one in which the new substance has very different properties from the old substance. Chemical changes happen in the real world all the time. Ask: What are some chemical changes that you use to change the properties of a material on a daily basis? *(Cooking food, washing dishes, eating)*

❹ Explain that in the industrial world, scientists are always experimenting with chemical changes to make new materials, such as *plastics*. Plastics are substances called *polymers*. Most polymers are made by mixing several different chemicals together, and each set of chemicals produces a polymer with different properties.

❺ Invite students to investigate how the properties of common substances change when they react to produce a simple polymer. Give each student a copy of the "Bouncing Glue Balls" lab sheet.

Bouncing Glue Balls

How do the properties of materials change when they undergo a chemical change?

❶ Put on your safety goggles. Fill the 6-ounce cup about $^3/_4$ full with water and add a teaspoon of borax. Stir until the powder dissolves. Observe the mixture and describe its properties below:

_____

_____

You'll Need

- safety goggles
- zipper-style sandwich bag
- teaspoon
- 6-oz paper or plastic cup
- 3-oz paper or plastic cup
- 20 Mule Team® borax detergent
- white glue
- water
- paper towels

❷ Next, carefully fill the 3-ounce cup with white glue. Observe the glue and touch it with your finger. How does it feel? Describe its properties below:

_____

❸ Hold the sandwich bag open and carefully pour all of the glue into the bottom of the bag. Next, pour in the borax-and-water mixture, being careful not to spill any. Zip the bag closed. Observe the two substances as they mix in the bag. Do you see any changes happening? Record your observations:

_____

_____

❹ Gently squeeze the bag to mix the glue with the borax-and-water solution. How does the mixture in the bag feel? How are the properties of the glue changing? Record your observations:

_____

❺ Based on the changes you have seen so far, what do you think will eventually happen to the mixture in the bag? Record your predictions here:

_____

❻ After about 10 minutes, carefully open the bag and remove the mixture. Rinse it off under cold water. Squeeze the glue into a ball and drop it on a table. How have the properties of the glue changed? Record your observations below:

_____

_____

Think About It: In this activity, you made a chemical change. How might this type of chemical change be put to practical use?

Sandwich Bag Science   Scholastic Teaching Resources

ALGER PUBLIC LIBRARY

Airlift Bag

Get It Together
- large round balloon
- "Need a Lift?" lab sheet (page 19)

Science in the Bag

Even though we don't normally see it, air is all around us! Air is a collection of gases, and gas, like other forms of matter, takes up space and has weight. When air gets moving it can power things like windmills. But even still air can do a great deal of work. When you ride in a car, you really are riding on air. The tires of the car are filled with air that has been put under pressure. Unlike solid or liquid, gas can be compressed, and the greater the pressure, the greater its potential to lift things up.

What to Do

❶ Inform students that they are going to investigate the power of air. Ask: What is air? *(A collection of gases)* Can air be used to make things move? *(Yes)*

❷ Invite a student volunteer to assist with a demonstration. Have the student blow up a balloon but not tie the knot. Ask the class to predict what will happen if the student lets the balloon go. *(The balloon will fly.)*

❸ Have the student release the balloon. Explain that the balloon flew because when it was inflated, the air inside was put under pressure. Unlike solids and liquids, gases can be compressed. The air that was trapped in the balloon was under greater pressure than the air in the room. As a result, when the balloon was released, the air inside flowed from higher pressure to lower pressure and escaped. In the process, it propelled the balloon across the room.

❹ Explain that compressed air can also do work even when it is not flowing. Challenge students to think of a way that a trapped volume of air can be put to work. Encourage them to think about the answer as you give each student a copy of the "Need a Lift?" lab sheet.

Need a Lift?

How can compressed air be used to move things?

You'll Need

- plastic straw
- large book (textbook or dictionary)
- table
- zipper-style sandwich bag
- cellophane tape

❶ Put one end of the straw in your mouth. Hold your hand in front of the other end and blow through the straw. What do you feel? Why? Write your ideas below:

_____

_____

❷ Place the book on the edge of a table or desk in front of you. Place one end of the straw between the book and the table. What will happen to the book when you blow into the straw? Write your prediction:

_____

_____

❸ Blow into the straw. What happens to the book? Why do you think that is?

_____

_____

❹ Remove the straw from under the book and place one end of it inside the sandwich bag. Zip the bag closed around the tip of the straw and then use the cellophane tape to completely seal the bag, making sure to tape the bag closed around the end of the straw. Place the bag with the straw between the book and the table. What will happen to the book when you blow into the straw this time? Write your prediction:

_____

_____

❺ Blow into the straw and observe the book. Record your observations below:

_____

❻ Based on your observations, explain why there was a difference between the two times you blew under the book. What do you think would happen if you used a bigger bag? Write your ideas below:

_____

_____

Think About It: Based on your experiment, can you explain how car tires work? Why do trucks and buses need to have bigger tires than cars and motorcycles?

Ice-Cube Race

Get It Together
- about 8 oz of modeling clay
- plastic knife
- metric ruler
- "On the Surface" lab sheet (page 21)

Science in the Bag

An object's *surface area* is the total area taken up by its entire outer surface measured in square centimeters or square inches. This is compared to an object's *volume*, which is the total amount of space within an object measured in cubic centimeters or cubic inches. Changing the shape or overall size of an object usually changes its surface area. In general, the smaller an object is, the larger the amount of surface area it has relative to its volume. Surface area comes into play during physical and chemical changes. Granulated sugar will dissolve much faster than a sugar cube because lots of little grains have a bigger total surface area compared to one large chunk.

Before You Start

Mold the modeling clay into a large cube, with each side about 4 cm long.

What to Do

❶ Take the cube of modeling clay and call on a student volunteer. Have the student use a ruler to measure and record the cube's length, width, and height. All three measurements should be the same.

❷ Ask: What is the volume of the cube? *(The number of cubic units it takes to fill a cube, found by multiplying the length by the width by the height; in this case, 64 cu. cm.)*

❸ Explain to students that while volume shows how many cubic units it takes to fill a cube, surface area refers to the number of square units needed to cover the entire surface of the object. Ask: What is the total surface area of the cube? *(Multiply the length by the width of one side, then multiply by 6; in this case, 96 sq. cm.)*

❹ Next, carefully slice the cube into eight equal-sized cubes. Ask: What happened to the total surface area of the cube? *(It doubled.)* Measure the surface area of each small cube and then multiply by 8, since there are now eight small cubes taking up the same space as the one large cube.

❺ Explain that by cutting up the cube you increased its surface area but kept the total volume the same. This important concept comes into play when matter undergoes chemical and physical changes. Often, changing the surface area of an object affects how fast a reaction happens.

❻ Invite students to investigate how a change in surface area can affect how fast a physical change takes place. Give each student a copy of the "On the Surface" lab sheet.

Name _____   Date _____

On the Surface

How does changing the surface area of an ice cube affect the rate at which it melts?

❶ Place an ice cube in each sandwich bag and zip each bag tightly closed.

❷ Take the hammer or rolling pin and gently break up the ice in one of the bags so that it is now in many small pieces. Be careful not to tear the bag! By crushing the ice, what did you do to the overall surface area of the cube?

_____

_____

You'll Need

- 2 zipper-style sandwich bags
- 2 same-sized ice cubes
- watch or clock with a second hand
- hammer or rolling pin

❸ Examine the ice in each bag. Which ice will melt faster? Why? Record your prediction and reasoning:

_____

_____

❹ Place the two bags side-by-side on a table in a warm room. Keep a close watch on the ice in the two bags. Every minute or so lift the bags to see how much of the ice has melted. Which bag of ice melted first?

_____

_____

❺ How did your observations compare with your prediction? Explain why you think you got the results that you did:

_____

_____

Think About It: How might you melt ice covering a sidewalk or street faster without using heat or chemicals?

Sandwich Bag Science   Scholastic Teaching Resources

Chromatography Bags

Get It Together
- plain white paper towels
- scissors
- 4 12-oz clear plastic cups
- red, green, and blue food coloring
- red apple
- water
- "Ink on the Run" lab sheet (page 24)

Science in the Bag

What color is black ink? Most people assume that it's black, but they're wrong! Black ink is really made up of many *pigments* blended together. To understand how this works, you must first understand that light is really made up of many different colors blended together. In the late 1600s, Sir Isaac Newton showed that "white" light (from the sun or a lamp) is really made up of several different colors, each with its own wavelength. If you take these same colors of light and put them back together again, you would wind up with white light.

Pigments (the things in ink or paint that give them their color) work in the opposite way. Pigments absorb all the wavelengths of light except for the color that you see reflected back. A red apple looks red because it reflects only the red wavelengths in light. If you start adding pigments together, eventually you will wind up with a pigment that absorbs all the wavelengths of light so none of the colors is reflected back. Result: The object will look black. Each pigment has its own unique physical and chemical properties. Scientists can use these differences to separate out different pigments from ink using a process known as *paper chromatography*. Basically, the way it works is that each pigment has its own density. If you suspend a strip of paper marked with ink in a container of water, the water will seep up through the paper, carrying the different pigments to different levels. The more pigments in the ink, the greater the color separation on the paper.

Before You Start

Cut the paper towels into 10-by-2-cm (4-by-1-in.) strips. Mix three drops of red food coloring into a clear 12-oz cup of water. Do the same for the blue and green food colorings so that you have three cups of different-colored water.

What to Do

❶ Hold up the apple and ask students: What color is the apple? *(Red)* Explain that even though the answer may seem obvious, there really is more to color than what we first see. For example, the apple looks red because it contains a pigment that reflects only red light back to our eyes. Pigments are things like dyes and paints. While red is a pure pigment, other pigments may be a combination of different colors mixed together.

(continued)

❷ Call for a student volunteer to assist you. Have the student hold up the cup with the red water and the cup with blue water. Ask the class to predict what will happen when the volunteer pours equal amounts of the red and blue water into a third cup. *(The resulting color should be purple.)*

❸ Have the volunteer mix the two colors into the empty cup until it's about half full. Compare the color in the third cup to the first two. Ask: What do you think will happen if we mix in some green water? *(The color will begin to look brown or black.)* Have the volunteer pour some green water into the third cup until it turns a muddy brown color.

❹ Explain that colors like brown and black are really a combination of many pigments mixed together. When manufacturers of paints and markers mix their pigments, they each have their own formula. Using a process called *paper chromatography*, we can separate different pigments in ink to see exactly what colors were used.

❺ Invite students to conduct their own experiment to discover the pigment blends used in three different brands of markers. Give each student a copy of the "Ink on the Run" lab sheet and demonstrate how to set up the chromatography bag.

Ink on the Run

Do all black inks contain the same pigments?

❶ Place a small piece of masking tape outside each sandwich bag.

❷ Use one of the black markers to write its brand name on the masking tape of one bag. Next, use the marker to draw a thin line across one end of a paper-towel strip, about 1 cm (½ inch) from the bottom. (See figure.) Staple the top of the paper strip to the top of the sandwich bag to hold the paper strip in place. The end of the strip with the line should touch the bottom of the bag.

❸ Repeat step 2 with the other two black markers, paper-towel strips, and bags. When finished, you should have three labeled sandwich bags with paper strips in them, each with a black line drawn using a different brand of marker.

You'll Need

- 3 zipper-style sandwich bags
- masking tape
- 3 different brands of black water-based markers
- 3 10-by-2-cm strips of white paper towel
- stapler
- cellophane tape
- medicine dropper
- water

❹ Look closely at the three lines drawn on the paper-towel strips. How do they compare with one another? Record your observations below:

_____

_____

❺ Tape each sandwich bag to a window or wall so that the three bags are lined up next to one another. Using the medicine dropper, put about 10 drops of water into the bottom of each sandwich bag so that the bottom of the paper-towel strip is resting in the water. Important: The black line should be above the water level.

❻ Wait a few minutes and then observe each of the paper-towel strips. What happens to the water? What about the black lines?

_____

_____

❼ After about 15 minutes, compare the three paper-towel strips. How are they similar? How are they different? Are all brands of black ink created the same? How do you know?

_____

_____

Think About It: How might you be able to tell which brand of marker was used to write a letter?

Sandwich Bag Science   Scholastic Teaching Resources

Crash Bags

Get It Together

- eggs
- roller skate or skateboard
- large smooth desk
- wooden meterstick
- 3-oz paper cup
- paper towels and sponge for cleanup
- "Crash Test" lab sheet (page 26)

Science in the Bag

Most new cars come packed with all sorts of safety equipment, but the two most important ones are seat belts and air bags. Some people think that air bags are designed to replace seat belts, but in reality they are designed to be used together. Consider Newton's first law of motion, which states that a body in motion will stay in motion unless an outside force acts upon it. If you are in a car traveling at 50 miles per hour, you are also moving at 50 miles per hour. If you suddenly hit the brakes, the force of the brake will stop the car, but you'll continue moving forward until you hit the windshield. This is where the seat belt comes in! It holds you tight to the seat to keep you from flying forward. But the sudden impact of the seat belt against the chest and shoulder coupled with the snap of the neck can also cause severe trauma. That's where the air bag comes in! It provides a cushion between the passenger and the front of the car. This reduces the seat belt's strain on the body and minimizes the snap of the neck. But without the belt to restrain you, slamming into an air bag can be almost as bad as hitting the car itself!

Before You Start

Hard-boil enough eggs so that each group of students will have two eggs. For maximum effect you might want to use a raw egg for the demonstration.

What to Do

❶ Ask students: What are air bags and seat belts for? *(To protect passengers in an accident)* Explain that air bags and seat belts help counter Newton's first law of motion, which states that a body in motion will stay in motion until an outside force acts upon it.

❷ Place the paper cup on top of a roller skate or skateboard, then place the egg in the cup. Slowly push the skate. Tell students: *Pretend that this egg is a person and the skate is a car. When I push the skate, both the skate and egg are in motion.* Ask: What would happen to the egg if the skate suddenly stopped? *(It would fly off.)*

❸ Ask a volunteer to hold a meterstick across the table. Shove the skate toward the meterstick and have the class observe what happens to the egg when the skate hits the meterstick. The egg should fly out of the cup and crash into the table. Explain that even though the skate stopped when it hit the meterstick, the egg stayed in motion.

❹ Challenge students to find out how seat belts used together with air bags help. Give each student a copy of the "Crash Test" lab sheet.

Name _____   Date _____

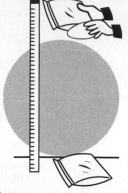

Crash Test

Why should you wear seat belts even when your car has air bags?

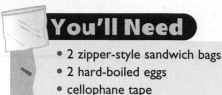

You'll Need
- 2 zipper-style sandwich bags
- 2 hard-boiled eggs
- cellophane tape
- meterstick

❶ Fill both sandwich bags with air and zip them closed. Place one sandwich bag on top of a desk, counter, or floor (without carpet). Hold a meterstick next to the inflated bag, making sure the stick points straight up in the air.

❷ Get ready to drop a hard-boiled egg and the other inflated sandwich bag together onto the first inflated bag. Before you do, predict what will happen to the egg when it hits the first bag. Write your prediction below:

_____

❸ Hold the inflated bag with the egg under it about a meter directly above the first inflated bag. Drop both items at the same time. What happened to the egg? Record your observations below:

_____

_____

❹ Take the second hard-boiled egg (or use the first egg if it didn't crack during the first test) and use tape to secure it to an inflated bag. Next, tape the second inflated bag to the other side of the egg so that the egg is sandwiched between the two bags. Predict: What will happen when you drop the egg this time?

_____

_____

❺ Hold the egg and sandwich bags a meter above the hard surface again and let it drop. What happened to the egg this time? Record your observations here:

_____

_____

❻ Based on your experiments, explain why it's important to wear seat belts even if your car has air bags.

_____

_____

Think About It: What other modifications might you try to make your air-bag crash test work even better?

Sandwich Bag Science   Scholastic Teaching Resources

Static Electricity Bag

Get It Together
- balloon
- shredded newspaper
- "Taking Charge!" lab sheet (page 28)

Science in the Bag

Anyone who has ever gotten a shock after walking across a carpet has had firsthand experience with static electricity. *Static electricity* is the result of an object either gaining or losing electrons. Electrons, which are found in all atoms, are present in all forms of matter. But not all types of materials hold on to their electrons the same way. Some materials, like fur and hair, give up some of their electrons very easily. These materials are known as *electron donors*. Other materials, like rubber and most plastic, grab on to extra electrons. They are known as *electron acceptors*. Whenever a substance gains or loses electrons, it becomes charged. If it gains extra electrons the charge is negative, and if it has lost electrons the charge is positive. When two objects with opposite charges are brought near each other, or if a negatively charged object is brought near an object with no net charge, they attract each other. By seeing how strong the force of attraction is, you can measure how well an object either gains or loses electrons.

What to Do

❶ Ask students: Have you ever gotten a shock after walking across a rug and touching a doorknob? What caused the shock? *(Static electricity)*

❷ Explain that people have been experimenting with static electricity for hundreds of years, but it wasn't until recently that scientists began to truly understand how it worked. Ask a student volunteer with relatively long hair to assist you. The hair should be clean, without gel, hair spray, or mousse.

❸ Place a small pile of shredded newspaper on a desk where the class can see. Blow up a balloon and tie a knot in it and begin rubbing the balloon on the volunteer's head. Ask students: What is the balloon removing from the hair? *(Electrons)* Have students predict what will happen when you hold the balloon above the volunteer's head. *(Hair will lift toward the balloon.)* Demonstrate what happens.

❹ Explain that the balloon is an *electron acceptor*—it readily accepts free electrons. Hair is an *electron donor*, readily giving away extra electrons. When the balloon got extra electrons from the hair, it became negatively charged while the hair became positively charged. When two objects with opposite charges come together, they attract.

❺ Rub the balloon on the volunteer's head again and hold it above the paper. Pieces of newspaper should jump up and stick to the balloon. Explain that the balloon has so much negative charge, that it even attracts the paper, which has no charge.

❻ Invite students to conduct their own experiment to discover which types of materials make the best electron donors. Hand out copies of the "Taking Charge!" lab sheet.

Name _____   Date _____

Taking Charge!

What types of materials produce the most static charge?

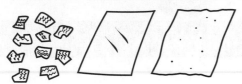

You'll Need

- zipper-style sandwich bag
- sheet of newspaper
- 30-cm piece of aluminum foil
- 30-cm piece of wax paper
- dry paper towel

❶ Tear the newspaper into tiny pieces about ½ cm (¼ in.) in size. Spread the pieces of newspaper on a clean, dry table.

❷ Place your hand inside the sandwich bag and hold it about 1 cm above the newspaper pieces. What happens to the paper?

_____

❸ Next, briskly rub your hand with the bag on your head or arm. What will happen when you bring the bag near the newspaper pieces this time? Write your prediction below and then try it. Was your prediction correct?

_____

_____

❹ Rub the bag against the palm of your other hand a few times to remove any static charge. Test it by holding the bag above the newspaper. The paper should not be attracted to the bag.

❺ See the list of materials below. Test how well each material builds up a static charge by rubbing it against the bag and then holding the bag over the newspaper pieces. The greater the material's static charge, the more the newspaper will be attracted to the bag. Before testing each material, predict whether you think it will have a big charge, little charge, or no charge. Then test the material and record your observations. After testing each object, discharge the bag by rubbing it against the palm of your hand.

Material	Prediction	Observation
Aluminum foil		
Wax paper		
Paper towel		
Your pants		
Your shirt		

Think About It: Based on your tests, what types of materials produce the most static charge?

Sandwich Bag Science   Scholastic Teaching Resources

Bernoulli Bag

Get It Together
- round balloon
- sheet of copier paper
- electric blow-dryer
- "Taking Off!" lab sheet (page 30)

Science in the Bag

What do boomerangs, Frisbees, and airplane wings have in common? Apart from the fact that they all fly, they all have the same general shape. If you look at any of them edge on, you'll find that they're curved on the top and relatively flat on the bottom. This isn't just a coincidence. This design helps maximize the amount of lift when these objects fly. The idea behind this lies in *Bernoulli's principle*, which says that when a stream of air moves over the curved top of a wing, it has to travel a greater distance than the air below the wing. The air above the wing gets "thinned out" compared to the air below. As a result, the air above the wing has lower pressure than the air below it. The higher pressure below the wing pushes it up, creating lift.

What to Do

❶ Take a poll by asking students how many of them have ever flown in an airplane. Ask: Has anyone looked closely at the wings? How are they shaped? *(Curved on top and flat at the bottom)*

❷ Explain that airplane wings tend to be curved on the top and flat at the bottom due to *Bernoulli's principle*. Back in the 1700s, Swiss scientist Daniel Bernoulli discovered that if you get a fluid to flow faster over the top of a surface than below it, the fluid below the surface will have more pressure and produce lift.

❸ Invite a student volunteer to assist you. Turn on the blow-dryer to low. Point it straight up in the air and ask the volunteer to hold a flat sheet of paper over the flow of air. Ask the volunteer to let the paper go. It will fly off and fall to the ground.

❹ Next, ask the volunteer to blow up the balloon and knot it. Turn the blow-dryer on again and point it up. Ask the volunteer to hold the balloon over the stream of air and let it go. By moving the blow-dryer back and forth slightly, you should be able to keep the balloon suspended in the flow.

❺ Challenge students to explain why the balloon floated and the paper fell. *(The answer lies in the curved shape of the balloon and the amount of air it displaces, not its weight.)* Explain that what they have just witnessed was Bernoulli's principle in action.

❻ Invite students to conduct their own test of Bernoulli's principle. Give each student a copy of the "Taking Off!" lab sheet.

Name _____   Date _____

Taking Off!

Does the shape of a wing affect how well a plane flies?

You'll Need

• zipper-style sandwich bag

❶ Take an empty sandwich bag and smooth it out to get all of the air out. Zip the bag closed. Grasp each end of the zipper part of the bag with your hands and hold the top of the bag against your chin, right below your lower lip. The bag should be hanging down in front of your chin.

❷ Predict: What will happen to the bag when you blow down on top of it? Write your prediction:

_____

_____

❸ Test your prediction by blowing down on top of the bag. What happened? Record your observations here:

_____

_____

❹ Now fill the bag with as much air as possible and zip it closed, making sure it is tightly sealed. How does the shape of the inflated bag compare to the empty bag? What will happen to the bag if you blow down on it this time? Write your prediction here:

_____

_____

❺ Holding the bag the same way as before, blow down on top of the inflated bag. What happens? Record your observations:

_____

_____

❻ How did the shape of the bag affect the way it behaved when you blew air over it? Based on your experiment, why do you think most airplane wings have a curved top?

_____

_____

Think About It: Can you think of any animals that benefit from Bernoulli's principle? How?

Sonic Insulation Bags

Get It Together

- dry sand
- water
- measuring cup
- 4 zipper-style sandwich bags (for each pair of students)
- cymbal or large metal mixing bowl
- wooden spoon or drumstick
- "Maximum Mufflers" lab sheet (page 32)

Science in the Bag

Sound is a form of energy. In order for sound to happen, something has to move or vibrate. Unlike light, which can travel through a vacuum, sound waves must move through some form of matter, like solid, liquid, or gas. How well sound waves travel through matter depends on the density of the matter. In general, the denser the matter, the more efficiently sound will travel through it. Blocking sound waves is the goal when soundproofing a room. In many cases, special tiles or foam rubber blocks are used because they contain many dead air spaces in them. As sound moves through these dead spots, vibrations slow down or stop altogether.

Before You Start

Pre-fill the sandwich bags with sand and water. For each pair of students, fill two sandwich bags with 8 ounces of dry sand and two bags with 8 ounces of water.

What to Do

❶ Grab students' attention by striking the cymbal (or mixing bowl) with the wooden spoon. Ask: How could you have blocked out this noise? After listening to some responses, explain to students that they will test out different materials to see which make the most effective sound barriers.

❷ Ask: What must you have to produce sound? *(Vibrations)* Explain that—unlike light, which can travel through a vacuum—sound needs to pass through something to get from one place to another, like solid, liquid, or gas.

❸ Invite the class to try this hands-on experiment: Have them take their right index finger and hold it about 5 centimeters (2 in.) away from their right ear. Using their left index finger, they should scratch their right index finger and listen for the sound it produces.

❹ Next, tell them to repeat the experiment, only this time they should touch their ear with the finger that is being scratched. Ask: What happened to the sound? *(It got louder.)* Explain that the sound became louder because your finger is solid, and solids transmit sound much better than liquids or gases. How well sound travels through a material depends on the physical properties of that material. A down pillow will stop a sound cold, while rock or steel will let sound waves travel for many miles.

❺ Challenge students to investigate which materials would make the best sound insulators. Give each student a copy of the "Maximum Mufflers" lab sheet.

Name _____   Date _____

Maximum Mufflers

What types of materials provide the best sound insulation?

❶ This activity is best done with a partner. Start by getting a relatively loud sound source such as an alarm clock, a radio, or a bell. Sit about 3 meters (10 ft) away from the sound source and listen to how loud it sounds.

You'll Need

- mechanical alarm clock, bell, or other device that produces a fairly loud sound
- 2 zipper-style sandwich bags, each with 8 oz of dry sand
- 2 zipper-style sandwich bags, each with 8 oz of water
- 2 zipper-style sandwich bags, each filled with air
- a partner

❷ Predict: Which do you think will make the best sound insulators— the bags filled with sand, the bags filled with water, or the bags filled with air? Write your prediction here:

_____

❸ Hold a bag of sand over each ear and listen to the sound again. Make sure that you are exactly the same distance away from the sound source as the first time. How did the sound compare to the first time? Record your observations:

_____

_____

❹ Repeat step 3, this time holding a bag of water over each ear. How did the sound compare to when you listened through sand? Was it louder, softer, or the same? Why do you think this was so?

_____

_____

❺ Repeat step 3, this time using the two bags filled with air. How did the sound compare to the other two times? Why do you think this was so?

_____

_____

❻ Based on your experiment, which type of matter seems to be best at insulating against sound? Explain your reasoning.

_____

_____

Think About It: Why do you think that acoustic insulation is often made with lots of air spaces in it?

Sandwich Bag Science Scholastic Teaching Resources

Sandwich Bag Still

Get It Together

- large glass of salt water (Mix one tablespoon of salt in a glass of water.)
- 8-oz clear plastic cup
- disposable coffee filter
- "Hold the Salt" lab sheet (page 34)

Science in the Bag

About 70 percent of our planet is covered with water. Unfortunately, almost 97 percent of that water is found in the ocean and is too salty to be used for most activities. As the population grows, our freshwater resources are becoming stretched to the limit. In some areas where freshwater is really scarce, people have begun using a process called *desalinization*, which removes salt from ocean water. While this process works well, it's quite expensive and energy intensive. The problem is, the salt in water is in solution so it can't be easily filtered out. The most effective way to remove salt is through *distillation*, where water is heated, turned into vapor, and then condensed back into liquid. In this process, all of the impurities, including salt, are left behind. Most stills use fossil fuels, like gas and oil, to heat water. Recent experiments using solar energy, however, have shown that it can be quite effective in purifying water, much like it does in the natural water cycle.

What to Do

❶ Hold up the glass of salt water and ask a student volunteer to come and taste the water by dipping a clean finger into the glass and placing the finger on his tongue. The student's reaction will indicate to the class that the water is salty.

❷ Explain that even though Earth is a wet planet, most of the water is not useable because it is in the ocean, and ocean water is salty. Holding up the glass, ask students if they can tell if the water is salty just by looking. (*No, because the salt is in solution so it's invisible.*)

❸ Encourage the class to think of ways to get the salt out of the water. If no one suggests filtering, ask students if they think salt can be filtered out of water.

❹ Ask another volunteer to hold the filter over the empty plastic cup. Slowly pour the salt water through the filter. Then ask the volunteer to test the filtered water by dipping in her finger and tasting it. The water will still be salty.

❺ Explain that because the salt is in solution, you can't separate it from water using simple filters. The best way to desalinate water is to *distill* it. Most *stills* boil water, capture the vapor, and then cool it down so it turns back to liquid. Stills are expensive to operate because they use a lot of energy to turn water into vapor.

❻ Remind students that we have a free energy source–the sun. Invite them to investigate how solar energy can purify salt water. Distribute copies of the "Hold the Salt" lab sheet.

Name _____   Date _____

Hold the Salt

How can the sun be used to purify water?

❶ Add 2 or 3 good shakes of salt to the water in the small cup and stir it until the salt dissolves completely. Look at the salty water in the cup. How does it look compared to freshwater? Dip a finger into the cup of water and touch it to the tip of your tongue. How does the water in the cup taste? Record your observations:

_____

_____

You'll Need

- zipper-style sandwich bag
- 3-oz cup of water (plastic bathroom cups work best)
- small stirring stick or coffee stirrer
- saltshaker
- a sunny spot (a windowsill works fine)

❷ Without spilling any water, carefully place the cup inside the sandwich bag and zip the bag closed. Place the sandwich bag with the cup in a sunny spot for at least 15 minutes. Predict: What do you think will happen to the water in the cup when it sits in the sun? Write your prediction here:

_____

_____

❸ After 15 minutes have passed, observe the plastic bag. Do you see any changes? What do you see? What do you think may have caused it? Write your ideas below:

_____

_____

❹ Carefully open the sandwich bag and remove the cup without spilling any water. Take your finger and rub it on the inside of the bag. Touch your finger to the tip of your tongue. How does the water in the bag taste compared to the water in the cup?

_____

_____

❺ Based on your experiment, explain how the sun's energy worked to purify the water. How might a device like this be used to make ocean water drinkable?

_____

_____

Think About It: How does this activity simulate the way the water cycle works in nature?

Sandwich Bag Science Scholastic Teaching Resources

Magnetic Sand Bag

Get It Together

- 1 pound of magnetic sand or iron filings
- zipper-style sandwich bags (one for each group of students)
- large magnet
- piece of paper
- box of steel paper clips
- "See the Force" lab sheet (page 36)

Science in the Bag

Every magnet, regardless of size and shape, has a *magnetic field*. This is the zone in which the magnet will exert a force on some magnetic material or another magnet. This field is concentrated at the two poles of the magnet. Lines of force extend from one pole to the other in arc-like paths. The stronger the magnet, the larger the field and the longer the magnetic lines of force are. While the field itself is invisible, it is possible to see the magnetic lines of force by using iron filings or magnetic sand. If you place a magnet on top of a bag filled with these particles and gently tap the bag, the particles will line up along the magnetic lines of force, making a map or picture of the field. Each type of magnet has its own unique field size and shape.

Before You Start

Iron filings can be purchased from most science supply stores. Magnetic sand actually works better and can be collected free at many beaches. Simply go to the beach with a strong magnet and a large zipper-style bag. Turn the bag inside out and place the magnet inside the inverted bag. Run the bag through dry sand and black magnetic sand will cling to the magnet right through the bag. When you have a large amount of sand on the magnet, carefully invert the bag again so that the sand will be inside the bag. Fill a sandwich bag for each group with about one ounce of sand and seal the bag.

What to Do

❶ Hold up a large magnet and ask students: What type of materials do magnets stick to? *(Iron and steel)* Use the magnet to test several different items in the room.

❷ Ask: Does a magnet actually have to touch an object to be attracted to it? *(No)* Invite a volunteer to assist you. Place several paper clips on a desk and cover them with a piece of paper. Ask the volunteer to place the magnet on top of the paper and slowly lift it. The paper clips should stick to the magnet through the paper.

❸ Explain that the magnet sticks to the paper clips through paper because every magnet has an invisible area around it called a *magnetic field*. Any magnetic material that comes within the field will be attracted to the magnet. In many cases, the magnetic field can go right through nonmagnetic materials, like paper.

❹ Tell students that they will investigate if the size and shape of the magnetic field change for different magnets. Distribute copies of the "See the Force" lab sheet to each student.

See the Force

How can you see a magnetic force field?

You'll Need

- about 1 oz of magnetic sand or iron filings in a zipper-style sandwich bag
- several different magnets

❶ Take a magnet and place it on top of the sandwich bag with the iron particles. What happens to the particles in the bag when they get near the magnet? What does this tell you about how the magnetic field works?

_____

_____

❷ Take off the magnet and lay the bag flat on a table. Slide it back and forth a few times to scatter the particles evenly around the bag. Select one magnet and gently place it on top of the bag near the center. Gently tap the tabletop next to the bag. What happens to the particles when the tabletop vibrates?

_____

_____

❸ After tapping on the table for several seconds, stop and look at the pattern that the particles make in the bag. This pattern is a map of the magnet's magnetic field. Draw a picture of the magnetic field on the back of this page. (Make sure to leave enough room for more drawings.)

❹ Now choose a different magnet. Repeat steps 2 and 3 with the second magnet. Draw the picture of its magnetic field on the back of this page below the first one. Repeat with another magnet.

❺ Based on your observations, what can you say about the shape of a magnet's force field? Do they all look the same?

_____

_____

❻ What factors might control the size and shape of a magnetic field?

_____

_____

Think About It: After conducting this experiment with several different magnets, do you think you can tell what a magnet looks like just by looking at a map of its magnetic field? How does the strength of a magnet compare to the size of the field it produces?

Sandwich Bag Science Scholastic Teaching Resources

Ocean Current Simulator

Get It Together
- clear 2-liter soda bottle (one for each group of students)
- ruler
- sharp scissors
- a world map or globe
- "Hot Stuff/Cold Stuff" lab sheet (page 38)

Science in the Bag
While ponds, lakes, and oceans may seem like homogeneous bodies of water, small currents often flow through them. These currents are often caused by the uneven heating and cooling of water. Water, like most forms of matter, becomes less dense when it gets warm. As a result, warm water tends to flow up toward the surface while cold water tends to sink. Scientists call this type of flow *convection*, and it affects all fluids, including air and molten rock (magma). Convection not only causes the motion in the ocean, but also makes the wind blow and the continental plates shift positions on Earth.

Before You Start
Remove the labels from the soda bottles. For each bottle, measure and mark about 20 centimeters (8 in.) from the bottom. Cut off the top of the bottle from the mark, leaving behind a plastic cylinder. Make sure you have access to hot tap water (around 100°–110° F.)

What to Do
❶ Ask students if they've ever gone swimming in the ocean or a lake when they suddenly hit a patch of warmer or colder water. Explain that these hot and cold spots are often caused by water currents. Ask students: What is a current? *(A flow of something, like electricity or water)*

❷ Hold up a globe or a world map, pointing to the Atlantic Ocean. Explain that currents are like rivers that flow through the ocean waters. In the Atlantic Ocean, one famous current is called the Gulf Stream. It flows up from the equator along the East Coast of the United States and across the north Atlantic toward England.

❸ Explain that many currents are caused by a process called *convection*. Convection is the flow of heat from one place to another within a fluid. Tell students that they will be conducting an experiment to observe what causes ocean currents. Distribute copies of the "Hot Stuff / Cold Stuff" lab sheet to students.

Hot Stuff/ Cold Stuff

How does convection drive ocean currents around the earth?

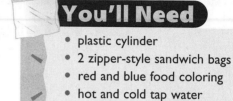

You'll Need

- plastic cylinder
- 2 zipper-style sandwich bags
- red and blue food coloring
- hot and cold tap water
- large rock
- sharp pencil or pen

❶ Place a few drops of blue food coloring into one sandwich bag and fill the bag with cold tap water. Zip the bag closed, squeezing out as much air as possible. Place the bag at the bottom of the empty cylinder and weigh it down with a large rock.

❷ Fill the cylinder with cold tap water. The bag should stay at the bottom. If it begins to float up, adjust the rock to hold it down.

❸ Prepare to puncture the bag with a sharp pencil. Predict: What will happen to the blue water when you put a hole in the bag?

_____

❹ Puncture the bag with the pencil point and observe what happens. Record your observations here:

_____

❺ Drain the water from the cylinder and remove the rock and bag. Empty the bag in a sink and throw it out. Place several drops of red food coloring in the second bag and fill it with hot tap water. Place the bag in the empty cylinder and put the rock on top to hold it down.

❻ Fill the cylinder with cold tap water and prepare to puncture the bag again. Predict: What will happen to the red water this time when you puncture the bag?

_____

❼ Puncture the bag with the pencil and observe what happens. Record your observations here:

_____

❽ Did the hot water behave the same way as the cold water? How were they the same? How were they different?

_____

_____

Think About It: How does this experiment explain why ocean currents move the way they do?

Sandwich Bag Science   Scholastic Teaching Resources

Air-Pressure Bag

Get It Together
- large, clean, hard plastic containers (e.g., large peanut-butter jar, 32-oz yogurt container, quart-size salad or soup container from a deli or Chinese takeout)
- clean toilet plunger
- "The Invisible Force" lab sheet (page 40)

Science in the Bag
Even though we don't normally feel it, air is always pushing down on us. In fact, at sea level, air pressure is almost 15 pounds per square inch. That means most of us are being weighed down by several hundred pounds of air. So why don't we feel it? In addition to the air pressing down on us from the outside, we have air inside us pushing back. For the most part, the air inside us counteracts and balances the air pressing from the outside. Occasionally we do get out of balance, like when we ride up and down in an elevator or drive up and down tall mountains. We feel our ears pop because as we change elevation, the air pressure changes. In this activity, students see just how much force air exerts on us.

Before You Start
Collect enough plastic containers so that each group will have one. Make sure that they are clean and that the container's opening is small enough so that a sandwich bag can fit over the top without ripping.

What to Do
❶ Take a clean toilet plunger and gently set it on a smooth desktop. Invite a student volunteer to lift the plunger. It should lift right off the desk with no problem.

❷ Ask students: What will happen if I push the plunger down on the desk really hard? *(It will stick to the desk.)*

❸ Press the plunger hard on the desk and invite another volunteer to remove it. The plunger should stick. Ask: Why does this happen? *(The plunger acts like a suction cup, so when you push it hard, it sticks to the desk.)*

❹ Explain that even though we call devices like plungers "suction cups," they don't really suck onto things. Instead, they are being pushed down by the air on top of them.

❺ Ask students if they have ever felt their ears "pop" when they go up and down a tall building or mountain. Explain that this popping is due to changing air pressure. Even though we can't see it, air has mass and is always pushing against us.

❻ Invite students to do their own test of air pressure. Give each student a photocopy of "The Invisible Force" lab sheet and demonstrate how to build the air-pressure bag.

The Invisible Force

How much force does atmospheric pressure have?

❶ Take the sandwich bag and place it inside the empty container. Spread the open end of the bag around the outer lip of the container, being careful not to rip the bag. Hold the bag in place with two rubber bands, as shown.

You'll Need

- zipper-style sandwich bag
- large, clean, hard plastic container
- 2 large rubber bands
- sharp pencil or pen

❷ Look inside the bag. What is the bag filled with?

_____

❸ Using two fingers, reach into the container and grasp the bag. What do you think will happen when you try to pull the bag out of the container? Write your prediction below:

_____

❹ Slowly pull the bag out of the container. What happens? What force is at work here?

_____

_____

❺ Take the sharp pencil and punch a small hole in the bottom of the sandwich bag. What do you think will happen when you try to pull the bag out of the container this time? Write your prediction below:

_____

❻ Grasp the bag with two fingers again and slowly pull the bag out of the container. What happens this time?

_____

_____

❼ How were the forces changed the second time you did the experiment?

_____

_____

Think About It: How does this experiment explain how a suction cup works?

Sandwich Bag Greenhouse

Get It Together
- flashlight
- thermometer
- "The Heat Is On" lab sheet (page 42)

Science in the Bag

A greenhouse stays warm even in the cold of winter, thanks to sunlight, which is made up of many different energy wavelengths. The energy we see, called *visible light*, is only a small part of a much larger band of energy called the *electromagnetic spectrum*. Other wavelengths include ultraviolet, infrared, gamma rays, and X rays. The glass of a greenhouse acts like a filter, letting visible light pass through while blocking out most of the other wavelengths. When visible light strikes an object inside the greenhouse, it is absorbed and the object begins to heat up. The warm object then radiates out infrared energy (heat), which cannot pass back through the glass. As a result, the inside of the greenhouse gets warm.

Before You Start

This activity can be done either as a hands-on activity in which students work in small groups or as a demonstration in which each student completes his or her own lab sheet.

What to Do

❶ Find out what students know about greenhouses. *(A greenhouse is a glass building used for growing plants in the winter.)* Explain that a greenhouse works because of the way sunlight behaves when it strikes an object.

❷ Invite a student volunteer to read the temperature on a thermometer. Record the temperature on the board. Ask the class to predict what will happen to the temperature if you shine a flashlight onto the thermometer. *(The temperature should rise.)*

❸ Ask the volunteer to turn on the flashlight and hold it a few inches above the bulb of the thermometer. After about a minute, turn off the flashlight and have the volunteer read the temperature again. The temperature should have gone up a few degrees. Ask: What caused the temperature to rise? *(The light shining on the bulb caused the temperature to increase.)*

❹ Explain that we actually get very little direct heat from the sun. Most of the energy that reaches the Earth's surface is in the form of visible light. When light strikes an object, the light energy is absorbed and turned into heat. The warm object then heats the air around it. This is why air closer to the ground is warmer than air high in the sky. A greenhouse makes use of this effect to keep plants warm in the winter.

❺ Invite students to investigate the greenhouse effect. Give each student a copy of "The Heat Is On" lab sheet.

The Heat Is On

How does a greenhouse work?

❶ Find a sunny spot on a table or windowsill, or set up an incandescent lamp on a table.

You'll Need

❷ Place one thermometer inside a sandwich bag and zip it closed. Make sure that there is some air inside the bag when you do this. Keep the other thermometer out. Read the temperature on each thermometer. They should be the same temperature (or very close). Record the temperature of the two thermometers below:

- zipper-style sandwich bag
- 2 small identical thermometers
- watch or clock
- a sunny spot or incandescent lamp

    Temperature of thermometer inside the bag: _____

    Temperature of thermometer outside the bag: _____

❸ Place the two thermometers side-by-side in the sunny spot or under the lamp. If you are using a lamp, make sure both thermometers are the same distance from the bulb. What do you think will happen to the temperature on the thermometers after 10 minutes? Write your prediction here:

_____

_____

❹ After 10 minutes, read the temperatures on the two thermometers. Record them below:

    Temperature of thermometer inside the bag: _____

    Temperature of thermometer outside the bag: _____

❺ Is there a difference in temperature between the two thermometers? Why do you think that is?

_____

_____

❻ Explain how this activity is a good model for the way a greenhouse works.

_____

_____

_____

Think About It: How does this experiment explain why a car parked in the sun in the winter feels hotter on the inside than on the outside?

Chemical Weathering Bags

Get It Together

- quartz and marble chips
- safety goggles
- 2 large, clear plastic cups
- baking soda
- teaspoon
- 4 oz of water
- 4 oz of vinegar
- paper towels
- "Where Acid Reigns" lab sheet (page 44)

Science in the Bag

One of the biggest environmental problems we face these days is *acid precipitation* or *acid rain*. When water vapor in clouds mixes with certain gases in the atmosphere, the resulting precipitation becomes acidic. Acids can react with and dissolve certain materials. While they barely react to minerals like quartz and feldspar, acids can damage rocks and minerals that contain *calcium carbonate,* such as seashells, marble, and limestone. The process in which acid precipitation reacts with calcium carbonate is called *chemical weathering*. This process impacts not only rocks in the ground but also statues and buildings made from limestone or marble.

Before You Start

You can get quartz and marble chips from most garden centers or building supply stores or from a science supply catalog. You will need one hour to complete the entire activity.

What to Do

❶ Inform the class that they are going to see one of the less-publicized effects of acid rain. Ask: What is acid rain? *(Acid rain results when some pollutants in the air mix with water vapor in clouds. The resulting precipitation is acidic.)*

❷ Explain that acids are chemicals that react with other chemicals. Some acids are extremely dangerous, but some, like lemon juice and vinegar, are actually edible. All acids have the potential to be corrosive, or eat away at some other materials.

❸ Invite a student volunteer to assist you, making sure she puts on safety goggles first. Take two empty plastic cups and have the student put two teaspoons of baking soda in each cup. Place the cups on a table near the front of the room.

❹ Have the student pour 4 ounces of water into the first cup. The baking soda should dissolve. Explain that water is chemically neutral and does not react with baking soda.

❺ Have the student pour 4 ounces of vinegar into the second cup. The baking soda will immediately foam up. Explain that vinegar is a weak acid that reacts to baking soda.

❻ Tell students that much of the precipitation falling on the ground these days has the same degree of acidity as weak vinegar. Ask: How do you think acid rain affects rocks, minerals, and rock monuments? Invite students to conduct their own test. Give each student a copy of the "Where Acid Reigns" lab sheet.

Where Acid Reigns

Does acid rain impact all rocks the same?

❶ Examine the three rock samples and briefly describe the properties of each sample below. Use a ruler to measure each sample and record its size.

You'll Need

- 3 zipper-style sandwich bags
- piece of chalk (limestone)
- small marble chip
- small quartz chip
- waterproof marker
- 3-oz paper or plastic cup
- white vinegar
- ruler

Chalk (Limestone):

_____

Marble:

_____

Quartz:

_____

❷ Based on your initial observations, which rock type do you think will be most resistant to the acid? Which do you think will react the most? Write your predictions below:

_____

❸ Label the three bags "limestone," "marble," and "quartz." Place each sample in its corresponding bag. Add 3 ounces of vinegar to each bag and zip each bag tightly. Observe each one carefully. Do you see any reactions? Record your observations:

_____

_____

❹ Place the three bags in a safe location and allow them to sit undisturbed for at least an hour. Then, observe the bags again. Record your observations below:

_____

_____

❺ Allow the bags to sit undisturbed overnight and observe them the next day. Which type of rock reacted most with acid? Which reacted the least?

_____

_____

Think About It: How does this experiment explain why buildings and statues made from limestone and marble are easily damaged by acid rain?

Sandwich Bag Science Scholastic Teaching Resources

Sandwich Bag Eyeball

Get It Together
- large magnifier
- flashlight
- "Eye Spy" lab sheet (page 46)

Science in the Bag

The way our eyes work is truly amazing! One critical component of the eye is the *lens*. A lens bends light. A *convex lens*, as in a typical magnifying glass, bends light rays toward a common point called the *focus*. When you look at an object, light enters your eye through the lens, which is convex. The light is focused onto the back of your eye on a layer of light-sensitive cells called the *retina*. The retina then gathers the information and sends it to the brain to be processed into an image. The lens of the eye is an elastic ball that can change shape. This helps because sometimes we look at faraway objects and sometimes we look at things close up. To keep all of them in focus, the lens has to constantly adjust its focal length. Muscles along the edge of the eye pull and stretch the lens, making it thinner and thicker.

What to Do

❶ Ask students: How many of you have used lenses today? Explain that if they have used their eyes, then they have used lenses because there is a lens built into every eyeball.

❷ Ask: What is a lens? *(A device that bends or refracts light)* Explain that lenses are found in many optical devices. Depending on a lens's shape, it can bend light rays to a point and bring them into focus, or it can spread light rays far apart.

❸ Hold up a magnifier. Explain that a magnifier is similar to the lens of your eye, except the magnifier has a hard, rigid lens, while the lens of your eye is soft and flexible. Both lenses, however, are *convex*, which means that the sides are curved outward. Convex lenses bend light toward a point called the *focus*, concentrating light.

❹ Darken the room and shine a flashlight toward a wall so that it makes a spot. Invite the class to watch the spot as you place the magnifier in front of the flashlight. Slowly move the magnifier back and forth. The spot of light should get brighter and dimmer. Explain that as you move the magnifier, you are changing the focal point of the light. The spot will be brightest when the beam is in focus.

❺ Turn the lights back on. Ask students to hold one hand in front of their faces so that they are staring at their palm. Now tell them to quickly look up to the other side of the room. Explain that as they change their view from near to far, their eyes adjust its focus. Ask: How do you think the lens does this?

❻ Invite students to find out by experimenting with their own model eyeball. Give each student a copy of the "Eye Spy" lab sheet.

Name _____   Date _____

Eye Spy

How does the lens in your eye focus light?

❶ Use a mirror to take a close look at one of your eyes. The lens is right below the outer covering of the eye, called the *cornea*. What is the shape of the lens in your eye? Is it curved inward or outward?

You'll Need
- zipper-style sandwich bag
- water
- mirror

_____

❷ Fill the sandwich bag with water and zip it tightly closed. Hold up the sandwich bag by the zipper top and examine it closely. How is the water-filled sandwich bag similar to the lens of your eye? How is it different? Record your observations below:

_____

_____

❸ Hold up the water-filled bag in front of one eye and look at an object across the room. How does it appear?

_____

❹ Predict: What will happen to an object that you are looking at through the bag if the shape and thickness of the bag changes? Write your prediction below:

_____

❺ Using both hands, hold the bag from the top and look through it again. Slowly stretch and squeeze the bag so that it gets thinner and thicker. What happens to the object you are looking at through the bag? Record your observations below:

_____

_____

❻ Your eye has a flexible lens, much like the bag of water. Based on your experiments, explain how you think the lens of your eye adjusts to change the focus from nearby objects to faraway objects.

_____

_____

Think About It: What do you think happens to the lens in a person's eye over time? How does this explain why some people need to wear corrective lenses?

Sandwich Bag Science   Scholastic Teaching Resources

Touch-Sensitive Bag

OBJECTIVE: **To demonstrate how sensitive the skin is in determining the nature of an object**

Get It Together

- coins, building blocks, or other small objects with distinctive shapes
- "Magic Touch" lab sheet (page 48)

Science in the Bag

Humans have five primary senses—sight, hearing, touch, taste, and smell. While sight and hearing are the two that we usually depend on the most, when these senses are lost or impaired, touch generally becomes our most important sense. Like all of our senses, touch involves a process called *biofeedback*. When we hold something in our hands, impulses from nerves under the skin send messages to our brain. The brain then interprets these signals and returns messages to our hands. In order for the sense of touch to work properly, skin needs to be in direct contact with an object. Bare skin is incredibly sensitive. Not only can we detect slight differences in temperature, our skin can sense tiny textural differences in objects that are impossible for our unaided eyes to see. Anyone who has ever worn gloves knows that once the skin is covered with even a thin layer of material, it loses a great deal of this sensitivity.

Before You Start

Get together a collection of small objects to serve as "mystery objects," but don't reveal them to the class in advance.

What to Do

❶ Tell the class that they are going to experience a little "sensory deprivation," but don't explain what that means. Ask for a student volunteer to assist you.

❷ Blindfold the volunteer (or simply have him close his eyes). Take a mystery object from the collection and hold it up for the entire class to see. Place the object in the volunteer's hand and ask him to describe how it feels. After he has finished describing it, challenge the volunteer to guess what the object is.

❸ After the volunteer has made his guess, have him remove his blindfold and reveal the object. Ask: What sense were you using to figure out what the object was when you were blindfolded? *(Touch)*

❹ Ask the class: Have you ever been in a situation where you could not see where you were going but had to feel your way along? Explain that like all of our senses, touch can help us gather information about our environment. Sometimes, however, our senses can't work to their full potential. When senses are purposely blocked or impaired, it's called *sensory deprivation*.

❺ Pass out the "Magic Touch" lab sheets and pair up students. Give each student three mystery objects to use, making sure not to reveal them to the partner. Invite students to conduct their own investigation into the world of sensory deprivation!

Name _____   Date _____

Magic Touch

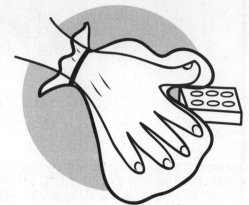

How important is bare skin to the sense of touch?

❶ In this activity, you will test to see how sensitive your hands really are and discover what happens when your senses are blocked. Have your partner put a hand inside the plastic bag. Use the rubber band to secure the open end of the bag around her wrist. Leave the other hand bare.

You'll Need

- gallon-size plastic storage bag
- large rubber band
- blindfold
- partner
- 3 small "mystery objects" (coins, buttons, building blocks, etc.) for each partner

❷ Place a blindfold over your partner's eyes or have her close her eyes. (Remind your partner that she's on the honor system!)

❸ Select a mystery object and write what it is on your partner's lab sheet, under the heading "Object." Place the object into your partner's covered hand and ask her to guess what the object is based on the way it feels. Record her guess on the lab sheet. Next, place the object in her bare hand and have her guess again. Record the second guess.

❹ Repeat steps 2 and 3 until you have done three mystery objects. Then switch places so that you will guess and your partner will record your answers. (Your partner should have a different set of mystery objects.)

Object	Guess (with hand in bag)	Guess (with bare hand)
#1:		
#2:		
#3:		

❺ Based on your experiments, what did having the bag on your hand do to your sense of touch? How did your ability to sense things change when you switched the object to your bare hand?

_____

_____

Think About It: What might be one of the biggest problems faced by technicians who have to wear protective gloves? How could they improve their situation?

Sandwich Bag Science Scholastic Teaching Resources

Sandwich Bag Seed Germinator

Get It Together
- large cup of dried lima beans
- large cup of lima beans that have been soaked in water for 24 hours
- toothpicks
- "Seed Racer" lab sheet (pages 51–52)

Science in the Bag

Most new plants begin their life cycle as seeds. While seeds come in many shapes and sizes, they all pretty much serve the same function. Inside the seed is a baby plant called an *embryo*. In addition, most seeds contain starchy material, which serves as nourishment for the young plant when it first starts to sprout. Most seeds have a tough outer covering called a *seed coat*, which protects the embryo until environmental conditions are just right for the seed to begin germinating. In many cases, the seed coat is so strong that, unless the seed is chewed and physically broken, it can pass through an animal's digestive system without being harmed. In fact, many plants use this process to disperse their seeds into new areas. Only when the seed coat has been subjected to enough moisture will it soften and fall away. In addition to moisture, other factors that control germination are temperature and soil chemistry. If conditions are right, the seed begins to germinate and the embryo begins to grow, feeding off the stored starch in the seed. From this point, it's a race for the baby plant to break through the soil and start photosynthesizing before it runs out of food in the seed.

Before You Start

About a day or so before conducting the lesson, soak about 50 to 60 large dried lima beans in a large cup of water. This way, the seed coats will be soft and easy to remove. This activity will require five days to complete so you might want to start it on a Monday.

What to Do

❶ Ask students if they have ever planted seeds in a garden. Did all the seeds sprout at the same time? *(Probably not)* Explain that seeds are actually pretty smart—they have a built-in mechanism that tells them when conditions are just right to begin growing. Since different plants live in different environments, it makes sense that each type of seed has its own special environmental cues.

❷ Give each student a dried lima bean. Encourage students to examine their seed. Ask: Is this seed living or nonliving? *(Living)* Explain that even though the seed looks hard, dry, and nonliving, it is only *dormant*. This means that it's in a state of suspension, waiting for the proper cues to start growing.

❸ Give each student one of the beans that have been soaking in water. Ask students to compare the wet seed with the dry seed. How are they different? *(The seed that was soaking is larger and softer and its outer covering is loose.)*

Sandwich Bag Seed Germinator

(continued)

❹ Explain that most seeds need enough water to get them soft before they can begin to germinate.

❺ Have students peel off the seed coat and use a toothpick to split the bean in two and expose the inside of the seed. Have them examine the seed closely. Explain that inside the seed is a baby plant called an *embryo*. In addition, the two large bean sections (called *cotyledons*) are full of starch. When the baby plant starts to grow, these provide nourishment until the plant breaks through the ground and starts making its own food through photosynthesis.

❻ Explain that because there are many different types of plants living in many different types of environments, each seed has its own unique set of trigger mechanisms that gets it to germinate. Some seeds require only moisture, while others may wait for the right temperature as well.

❼ Invite students to investigate which seeds germinate fastest under a specific set of conditions. Give each student a copy of the "Seed Racer" lab sheet and demonstrate how to build the birdseed germination bag.

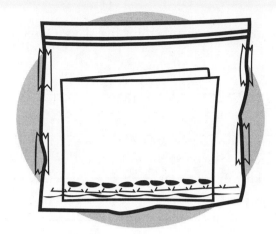

Seed Racer

Which type of seed will germinate the fastest under given conditions?

❶ Make your seed germination bag: Take a sheet of paper towel and fold it into quarters. Slip the folded towel into the sandwich bag and staple across the width of the bag about 2 cm (1 in.) up from the bottom. Set the staples right next to each other.

You'll Need

- zipper-style sandwich bag
- 2 plain white paper towels
- stapler
- small cup of wild birdseed
- 3-oz cup of water
- cellophane tape

❷ Pour some wild birdseed onto the second paper towel. Select three different types of seeds and describe each type of seed, including its name if you know it.

Seed # 1: _____

_____

Seed # 2: _____

_____

Seed # 3: _____

_____

❸ Pick four samples of each seed (so you have 12 seeds altogether) and place them inside the seed-germination bag so they rest on top of the staples. The seeds should be sandwiched between the bag and the paper towel. Spread them out so they are not crowded together.

❹ Based on your observations, do you think the seeds will all germinate at the same time? Why do you think so? Write your predictions below:

_____

_____

❺ Take the cup of water and slowly pour it into the bag. The water should seep through the staples and settle at the bottom of the bag. Some water may leak out of the staples. Stop pouring when the water comes up to the staples.

❻ Zip the bag closed, then tape it to a wall or window. Leave the bag undisturbed for five days. Observe the bag each day and record your observations:

Day # 1: _____

_____

Day # 2: _____

_____

Day # 3: _____

_____

Day # 4: _____

_____

Day # 5: _____

_____

❼ Did all the seeds germinate at the same time? Did all seeds of the same type behave the same way? What can you conclude from this experiment?

_____

_____

_____

Think About It: Besides water, what other factors might control which type of seed germinates first? How could you test these other factors?

Moldy Matters

Get It Together

- 4 or 5 slices of whole wheat bread without preservatives
- plastic bag
- zipper-style sandwich bags
- plant mister or spray bottle with water
- magnifiers
- "Moldy Matters" lab sheet (pages 55–56)

Science in the Bag

Even though most people don't appreciate it, mold is a very interesting form of life. Mold belongs to the kingdom *Fungi* and is classified as a *decomposer*. Unlike plants that produce their own food via photosynthesis, fungi live off other organic material, breaking it down into simpler chemicals. Most molds consist of long threadlike structures called *hyphae*, often forming a tangled mass called a *mycelium*, and reproduce by spores. When a mold spore comes in contact with some suitable organic material, it germinates and a *hypha* begins to grow into the material. As the hypha grows, it begins to branch out, creating a whole network of filaments that extend not only up into the air, but deep into the organic material. The hyphae extract nutrients, air, and water from the environment, continuing to grow until all of the organic material has decomposed.

Mold grows best in dark, moist habitats but it can tolerate a wide range of temperature and moisture conditions. It generally thrives in warm temperatures, but anyone who has ever left fruit in a refrigerator too long knows that even in cold temperatures, mold can grow. While mold is considered a problem because it spoils food, it is an important part of the biological world. Without mold, nutrients would not be fully recycled. While some molds can make people sick, they can also provide medical assistance. Remember, penicillin was discovered through mold!

Before You Start

You'll need to start creating moldy bread about two weeks before you conduct this activity. The best type of bread to use is whole wheat without preservatives. Lightly spray four or five slices with water from a plant mister and loosely wrap the bread in a plastic bag. Place the bag in a warm dark place. When you are ready to use the bread in class, place each slice in its own zipper-style sandwich bag. Seal the bags tightly to prevent the mold from circulating in the air in the class.

This activity will take about two weeks to complete. You will also need access to a refrigerator, or students can bring the bread home to store in their own refrigerators.

Moldy Matters

(continued)

What to Do

❶ Ask students if they have ever had some food turn moldy. Ask: What is mold? *(A type of fungus)* Some students may mistakenly think that mold is a plant. Explain that mold is a fungus and that fungi are not plants, but organisms that live off dead or dying organic material. Ask: Besides mold, can you think of any other type of fungus? *(Mushrooms, yeast, etc.)*

❷ Ask: What role do you think molds play in our ecosystem? *(Decomposers)* Explain that while molds may be a problem for people who buy and sell food, they are critical members of many ecosystems. Without fungi to break down dead organic material, nutrients would not be available for new living things!

❸ Divide the class into small groups and give each group a magnifier and a sealed sandwich bag with a slice of moldy bread in it. Tell students to observe the mold closely through the bag but warn them not to open it. Ask: What does the mold look like? *(It has lots of little threadlike filaments and some dustlike particles.)* Explain that the threads are called *hyphae* and they actually grow down into the organic material, taking nutrients from it. The dustlike particles are *spores*, which help molds reproduce. A spore is like a seed that germinates when it comes in contact with the right type of material.

❹ Explain that people in the food industry work hard to keep molds away. In many cases they add preservatives to food or spray crops with *fungicide*, chemicals that stop mold from growing. Even without fungicide, however, you can slow the growth of mold by making their environment less hospitable.

❺ Encourage students to find out under what conditions molds grow best. Give each student a copy of the "Mold Maker" lab sheet.

Mold Maker

What conditions are best for the growth of mold?

You'll Need

- 3 zipper-style sandwich bags
- 3 slices of preservative-free bread
- shoe box with lid or large coffee can with lid
- refrigerator or cooler
- masking tape
- marker

❶ You will need approximately two weeks to complete the entire experiment. Start by taking three slices of preservative-free bread that have all come from the same package. Place each slice in a zipper-style sandwich bag. Seal each bag tightly. Why is it best to use bread that has no preservatives in it? Why are you using bread that comes from the same package? Why are you sealing the bags? Write your ideas here:

_____

_____

_____

❷ Place a piece of masking tape on each of the three bags. Use a marker to label the first bag "Control," the second bag "Cold and Dark," and the third bag "Warm and Dark."

❸ Place the bag labeled "Control" in a safe place, such as on top of a shelf or bookcase. Place the bag labeled "Cold and Dark" in a refrigerator or cooler. Place the bag labeled "Warm and Dark" in a shoe box or large coffee can with a lid and put it near a radiator or window where it stays warm. What do you think is the purpose of the "Control" bag?

_____

_____

❹ Based on your knowledge of molds, which slice of bread do you think will get moldy first? Write your prediction and reasoning below:

_____

_____

(continued)

❺ Observe each of your bread slices over 10 days. Record your observations on the chart below:

Day	Control	Cold and Dark	Warm and Dark
1			
2			
3			
4			
5			
6			
7			
8			
9			
10			

❻ Based on your observations, under what conditions does mold grow best? If you want to keep bread fresh, where would you store it?

_____

_____

Think About It: In this experiment, you sealed the bread into three plastic bags. Where did the mold spores come from to make the mold grow?

Bags of Yeast

OBJECTIVE: To explore conditions under which yeast is most active

Get It Together
- bottle of apple juice
- bottle of nonalcoholic sparkling cider
- several clear plastic cups
- 4 or 5 packets of dry yeast
- white paper
- magnifiers
- "Rise and Shine" lab sheet (page 58)

Science in the Bag
Yeast, like mold and mushrooms, belongs to the kingdom *Fungi*. Over time, people found that they could use yeast in the wine-making, beer-brewing, and bread-baking industries. Without yeast, bread would be flat and hard, and drinks like sparkling wine and beer would not have bubbles! Yeast is a microscopic one-celled organism that feeds by causing a chemical reaction in sugars, breaking down the sugar to produce alcohol. That's why they are used in brewing beer and making wine. As yeast "eats," it releases carbon-dioxide gas, resulting in bubbles. These bubbles cause bread dough to rise when yeast is used for baking. Yeast thrives when it is warm and wet and has some type of sugar to consume.

Before You Start
If you prefer not to buy sparkling cider, make your own fermented apple juice by opening a bottle of juice and storing the open bottle in a warm place for about two weeks.

What to Do
❶ Divide the class into small groups. Ask students: What happens to apple juice when it gets old? *(It goes bad or ferments.)*

❷ Pour a few cups of apple juice for the class to pass around. Have students closely examine the juice, but not drink any! Ask: What properties does the juice have? *(It has a clear golden color, and it smells sweet.)*

❸ Next, pour a few cups of sparkling cider and pass them around, asking students to examine them as well. Ask: How is this liquid different from the first? *(The cider doesn't smell as sweet as the juice, and it has lots of bubbles.)*

❹ Explain that the cider started as regular apple juice, but over time it fermented, thanks to a tiny organism called *yeast*. Yeast is used to make beer, cider, wine, and bread.

❺ Give each group a packet of yeast. Have students open the packet and sprinkle some of the yeast onto a piece of white paper. Ask them to observe the yeast closely with the magnifier. What does it look like? *(Small, dry, brown particles that look like dust)*

❻ Ask: Is the yeast a living thing? *(Yes)* Explain that the yeast is alive, but dormant. Like all living things, yeast prefers certain environmental conditions in which to live.

❼ Invite students to investigate under which conditions yeast is most active. Give each student a copy of the "Rise and Shine" lab sheet.

Rise and Shine

Under what conditions is yeast most active?

❶ Label the first bag "Cold Water–Sugar," the second bag "Cold Water–Plain," the third bag "Warm Water–Sugar," and the last bag "Warm Water–Plain." Based on the labels, what factors will you be testing for in this experiment?

_____

You'll Need

- 4 zipper-style sandwich bags
- marker
- 4 packets of dry active yeast
- 2 packets of sugar
- measuring cup
- cold water
- warm water
- watch or timer

❷ Empty a packet of yeast and a packet of sugar into the bag labeled "Cold Water–Sugar." Pour in exactly 100 ml (3.4 oz) of cold water. Squeeze air out of the bag and zip it tightly closed. Check the watch and write the start time on the bag's label.

❸ Empty a packet of yeast into the bag labeled "Cold Water–Plain," and pour in exactly 100 ml (3.4 oz) of cold water. Squeeze air out of the bag, zip it closed, and write the start time on the bag's label.

❹ Repeat steps 2 and 3 with the two remaining bags, only this time use warm water instead of cold.

❺ Predict which bag will produce the strongest reaction. Which will have the least reaction? Why?

_____

❻ Wait exactly 10 minutes from the start time for each bag and then observe any changes in the bags. Write your observations on the data chart under "10 minutes." Continue observing every 5 minutes until 30 minutes have passed. Record your observations on the chart.

	10 minutes	15 minutes	20 minutes	25 minutes	30 minutes
Cold Water – Sugar					
Cold Water – Plain					
Warm Water – Sugar					
Warm Water – Plain					

❼ Based on your observations, under which set of conditions was the yeast most active? Which conditions produced the least reaction? Why do you think this was the case?

_____

_____

Think About It: In this experiment, you tested only two factors. What other environmental conditions might you be able to test? How would you set up those experiments?

Sandwich Bag Science Scholastic Teaching Resources

Transpiration Bags

Get It Together
- 3 small plants of different varieties (for each group of students)
- live specimens or photos of a cactus, a tomato seedling, and a fern
- fresh spinach leaves
- magnifiers
- "Water World" lab sheet (page 60)

Science in the Bag
Most plants need to be watered on a regular basis in order to stay healthy. Water is used in photosynthesis to make food for the plant. It also transports minerals, nutrients, and food throughout the plant. Much of the water that a plant takes in at its roots is lost back out through its leaves in a process called *transpiration*. Transpiration helps keep the plant cool and helps concentrate essential elements inside the plant tissue. The underside of a leaf has tiny openings called *stomata*, which allow gases to pass in and out of the plant. This is where most transpiration takes place. The topside of the leaf has no openings, and, in most cases, is covered with a thick waxy layer called the *cuticle*. This layer prevents too much transpiration from taking place. Not all plants transpire at the same rate. In fact some plants, like cacti, transpire very little. This makes sense because they live in a desert environment.

Before You Start
Obtain plant samples from a garden supply store or nursery several days beforehand and bring them into school so that they can adjust to the climate. Make sure the plants are small enough to fit inside a sealed gallon-sized plastic storage bag. Keep the plants in a sunny spot or under a grow light and water them daily. Do not water the plants on the day of the activity.

What to Do
❶ Hold up the three plant samples or photos of different plants. Ask students: Do these plants need the same amount of water to survive? *(No)* What factors might control how much water a plant needs? *(Local temperature, rainfall, root system, size of leaves, etc.)*

❷ Explain that water is a critical element for all plants. Not only does it transport nutrients within the plant, it also helps keep them cool. On hot days, water evaporates off the leaves in a process called *transpiration*.

❸ Pass out the spinach samples and magnifiers to students. Have them examine the two sides of the leaf closely. Ask: How does the topside of the leaf compare to the bottom? *(The topside is smooth and darker and feels a little waxy. The bottom is rough and has little holes.)* Explain that most plants' leaves are designed to minimize water loss. The tiny openings, called *stomata*, act like the pores in your skin.

❹ Ask: Do you think all plants transpire the same amount? Invite students to discover the answer as you hand out copies of the "Water World" lab sheet.

Name _____   **Date** _____

Water World

Do all plants transpire at the same rate?

❶ Examine the three plant specimens, looking closely at the tops and bottoms of the leaves. Write your observations below. If you know the name of the plant, include it in the description.

Plant # 1: _____

Plant # 2: _____

Plant # 3: _____

You'll Need

- 3 gallon-sized zipper-style storage bags
- 3 small plants of different varieties
- sunny spot or grow light
- watch or timer

❷ Based on your observations, do you think that all three plants will transpire at the same rate? Why or why not? Write your ideas below.

_____

_____

❸ Put each plant inside a bag and zip the bag closed. Place the plants in a sunny spot or under a grow light and wait at least 30 minutes. Why do you think the plants have to be in the sun? Why do the bags have to be sealed? What should you see forming inside of the bag?

_____

_____

❹ After 30 minutes, look at the three bags. Record your observations below.

_____

_____

❺ Do all the bags have the same amount of moisture collecting on the inside? What does this tell you about the way different plants transpire? Record your conclusions here:

_____

_____

Think About It: Why do you think cacti are well suited for living in a desert environment?

Sandwich Bag Science Scholastic Teaching Resources

A Salty Situation

Get It Together
- large plastic cup of water
- salt
- "Salt of the Earth" lab sheet (page 62)

Science in the Bag

If you've ever walked along a beach or the edge of a salt marsh, you've probably noticed that there are definite zones where only certain types of plants grow. While water is essential to plants, most plants have very specific tolerances when it comes to how much salt that water has. If you tried to grow a freshwater plant, like a tomato, along the edge of the ocean, it would die quickly. The same would be true if you attempted to grow seaweed in freshwater. Plant cells are filled with a liquid called *cytoplasm*, which is mostly water with a low concentration of salt. The *cell membrane* keeps the cytoplasm in, but it is permeable so that gases, nutrients, and water can flow in and out. This process of passive transport through the cell membrane is called *diffusion*. Under normal conditions there is no net loss of water from the cells because the concentration of salt in the water on either side of the cell membrane is about the same. If you take a freshwater plant and place it in salt water, however, the concentration of salt on the outside is much greater, so water flows out of the plant to even it out. As a result, the cells begin to collapse and the plant quickly wilts. The leaves get soft and mushy and lose their color. Unless the freshwater balance is restored quickly, the plant will die.

What to Do

❶ Hold up the cup of water and ask: Who would like a nice drink of cool water? Call on a volunteer, but before giving her the water, pour in a large quantity of salt. Ask: Do you still want that drink? (Even if the student says yes, don't let her drink it!)

❷ Ask if anyone has accidentally swallowed some salt water while swimming in the ocean. Usually when this happens, people get sick to their stomach and vomit. Your body has a natural defense system against drinking too much salt water, but why? What happens if you drink too much salt water? *(You can become extremely ill and even die.)*

❸ Explain that even though we have salt water in our bodies (e.g. blood, sweat, and tears) our bodies cannot tolerate too much salt. That's because our cells contain water, and if the concentration of salt inside and outside the cells is very different, the imbalance causes major disruptions in our bodies.

❹ Ask: What about plants? Can they tolerate salt water? *(Some can.)* If students say no, point out that salt marshes are full of plants that can grow in salt water!

❺ Ask: Do you think house plants or vegetables can tolerate salt water? Give each student a copy of the "Salt of the Earth" lab sheet to find out.

Salt of the Earth

What happens to freshwater plants when they are placed in salt water?

❶ Label one bag "Salt Water" and the other bag "Freshwater."

❷ Examine the two leaves closely. They should look fairly similar. Describe the condition of the leaves below, especially noting their color and how they feel (limp, firm, soft, etc.).

_____

_____

You'll Need

- 2 zipper-style sandwich bags
- 2 fresh romaine lettuce or spinach leaves
- water
- 6-oz plastic or paper cup
- 3 tsp salt
- marker
- plastic teaspoon

❸ Fill the bag labeled "Salt Water" with 6 ounces of water. Add salt to the water and zip the bag closed. Shake the bag a few times until most of the salt dissolves. Carefully open the bag and put in a leaf. Zip it closed and put it in a safe place. Make sure the leaf is submerged in the water.

❹ Fill the bag labeled "Freshwater" with 6 ounces of water. Place the second leaf in this bag and zip it closed. Put it in a safe place, making sure the leaf is submerged in the water.

❺ Predict: What do you think will happen to the two leaves? Write your prediction below:

_____

❻ After an hour, retrieve the two bags. Open the "Freshwater" bag and remove the leaf. How does it look compared to before it went into the bag? Record your observations below:

_____

_____

❼ Now open the "Salt Water" bag and take out the leaf. How does this leaf compare to before it went into the bag? Place it next to the other leaf for comparison. Record your observations below:

_____

_____

❽ Based on your observations, what would happen to a freshwater plant that was repeatedly watered with salt water? How could you further test your hypothesis?

_____

_____

Think About It: What do you think might happen to lawns and gardens in coastal communities if sea levels were to continue to rise?

Sandwich Bag Science Scholastic Teaching Resources

Sandwich Bag Stomach

OBJECTIVE: To investigate how your stomach aids in digestion

Get It Together

- large drawing or model of the human stomach
- football
- piece of chalk
- large, clear plastic cup
- vinegar
- "The Big Squeeze" lab sheet (page 64)

Science in the Bag

The human stomach, one of the major organs of the digestive system, is a thick-walled muscular sac responsible for much of the chemical and mechanical breakdown of food. Millions of microscopic *gastric glands* surround the inner lining of the stomach. These secrete *gastric juice*, a highly acidic liquid full of enzymes that chemically attack the food. But it's the stomach muscles that really make a difference. As these muscles contract, they churn and mash the food, creating a soupy mixture called *chyme*. After about four hours or so, the chyme is pushed by muscular contractions toward the *pyloric sphincter*, a tiny muscular ring that separates the stomach from the small intestine. The chyme is then pushed into the small intestine where further digestion and absorption of nutrients and water take place.

Before You Start

Try to obtain a drawing or model of the human digestive tract so students can visualize where the stomach is located and what it looks like.

What to Do

❶ Hold up the football and ask students: What part of your digestive system most closely resembles a football in shape and size? *(Stomach)* Explain that the stomach is a major organ of the digestive system, helping break down food so that nutrients can be absorbed by the body.

❷ Refer to the model or drawing of the human digestive system. Point to the stomach and explain that it is a muscular sac that can stretch to hold about one liter of food.

❸ Explain that the stomach breaks down food in two important ways. First, inside the stomach is a liquid called *gastric juice*, which is highly acidic and filled with chemicals called *enzymes*. Ask: What do acids do? *(Burn, corrode, or break down things)*

❹ Place a small piece of chalk in the bottom of a cup and fill the cup about halfway with vinegar. The chalk should start bubbling as it reacts with the acid. Explain that the acid in your stomach is about 10,000 times stronger than vinegar.

❺ Explain that the second way the stomach digests food is strictly mechanical. Muscles in the stomach help mash the food, producing a pulpy mixture called *chyme*.

❻ Invite students to find out how effective stomach muscles are in digestion. Give each student a copy of "The Big Squeeze" lab sheet.

Name _____   **Date** _____

The Big Squeeze

ALGER PUBLIC LIBRARY

How do the muscles around your stomach aid in digestion?

❶ In this activity, you will test to see how the muscles in your stomach assist in the digestive process. You will compare two bags, one with simulated muscular contractions and the other without. Which bag do you think will show the greater amount of digestion? Why? Write your prediction and ideas below:

WITHDRAWN

_____

_____

You'll Need

- 2 zipper-style sandwich bags
- 6-oz cup
- water
- watch or timer
- assortment of shelled peanuts, crackers, lettuce leaves, and other food stuff

❷ Take one sandwich bag and fill it with 6 ounces of water. Add a variety of food items, being careful not to overfill the bag. Zip the bag closed and make note of the time.

❸ Observe the contents of the bag and record your initial observations under "No Muscular Action." Place the bag off to the side and check it again in 5 minutes. Try not to move the bag too much as you make your observations. Record your observations every 5 minutes up to 15 minutes.

Observations	No Muscular Action	With Muscular Action
Initial		
After 5 minutes		
After 10 minutes		
After 15 minutes		

❹ Repeat step 2 with the second sandwich bag. This time, after zipping it closed, gently squeeze the bag five times, making sure not to rip or accidentally open it. Make note of the time.

❺ Observe the contents of the bag and record your initial observations under "With Muscular Action." Place the bag off to the side and check it again in 5 minutes. Each time you check the bag, squeeze it five more times. Record your observations every 5 minutes up to 15 minutes.

❻ Which bag showed the greater amount of breakdown? Why do you think this was so?

_____

_____

❼ In both cases, did all the food break down in 15 minutes? What does this tell you about the digestive process?

_____

_____

Think About It: In this experiment, you used just plain water to simulate the gastric juice of the stomach. How might you make the simulation more realistic?

Sandwich Bag Science Scholastic Teaching Resources